Quiet

The Spirit Catchers

Fate Unwritten (*Moving Mountains, book 1*)

Roads Untraveled (*Moving Mountains, book 2*)

Quiet

Poems about love, loss & healing

ISBN: 979-8-6834299-8-0

CONTENTS

Borrowed Time

I'm an artist
The world is my canvas and my subject
If Mother Earth were a model, how would you paint her?
She is aged and ageless
Unlike words, whose origins can be traced
But like all canvases, even time has its limits
Seconds, minutes, hours, and eras
Everything that is bold enough to exist
Must eventually be humble enough to die
I'm an artist
But I work on borrowed time
Carving temporary meaning
From the permanent mayhem
I'm an artist
But my tools belong to someone else
To the air into which they fade
Or the masses that glean them in passing
Not reading so much as seeing
As they are in the habit of doing with Mother Earth
I'm an artist
But my craft, like the Earth, is dying
Scarred by indifference
Polluted by ignorance
Withered by neglect
So I tend to it daily
Sowing the seeds of my curiosity
Hoping one day
They will bloom.

The lights dim
And you appear
Sublime and unassuming
Sprouting intrepidly from the cracks
Into which you slipped
Like a desert flower thirsting for rain
There's a science to love
And an art to staying sane
And where these worlds collide
I find you
Pulling me in
Alone together, we dance
Serenaded by the tender rhythm
Of silent songs and whispered dreams
I've been here before
But never like this
You are the river thundering through me
Content with your own company
And the duality of your power
The power to carry me gently
Or crush the air from my lungs
A dangerous dance
That ends
In a fall.

People want puddles, not oceans
To see their own reflection
Rather than limitless potential
They want knowledge, not understanding
In the same way
They yearn for dew drops on grass
But not the rain that feeds it
Don't they know
The lake only glitters on the surface
Where fish refuse to feed
For the same reason
The doe falters at the edge of the forest
For she is magnificent
And beautiful things demand to be seen
So she lingers
Ghosting through the woods
Under the cover of all that is predictable
And lackluster
For that's what people say
About things that refuse to shine
Don't they know
That glass, before it shimmers,
Runs through your fingers as sand
And flowers, before they bloom,
Take root in the dirt beneath your feet
Don't they know
Beauty is never a means to an end
But an end in itself

That ivory elephant on your credenza
Hardly does the real one justice
But people want statues, not elephants
And power without accountability
So they plunder and pillage and kill
Just to turn around and say,
"Isn't it beautiful?"

Lie with me, but don't speak
I don't want words
Brittle ambiguity studding the otherwise faultless silence
The absence of words is the perfect substitute for them
An endless cycle of catching breath
And releasing fear
Manufacturing language and ways to harness its potential
Pulling it from the silence it begs to fill
Just to say what's already been said
Every presence stems from an absence
As light does from darkness
As love does from loneliness
And words from silence
Lie with me. Say nothing.
I want to hear it all
The tempo of your heart
Marching tirelessly to its own beat
As the doe-eyed ballerina
Twirls in the music box
The rush of skin on skin
Like wind giving chase to clouds
Even the wind despairs against the silence
And so it whistles and howls and roars
And when we hear nothing
When the sky is still and the air is dead
I think of you and the holes you fill
Like sunlight in treetops
Or echoes in caves

Reminding me, always,
Of the silence.

Swinging at the edge of insanity
Above a long drop into despair
The cold clinch of oblivion beckons you
You say you're sorry
As you fall into my arms
I can't tell
If I'm pushing you away
Or pulling you in
And just when I think
You've finally stopped swinging
When the chains that hold you are silent and still
You step off with both feet
And begin again
Isn't it funny
How the smallest gestures have the greatest impact?
Like my hand on your back at rock bottom
Keeping you grounded
Or killing us both
You shrink from my attempts to save you
Flying into the face of danger
Then diving backwards into defeat
Where I wait to catch you again.

I see myself in all the things I am not
The bold, brave lines of a well-defined thought
Like a smile on a stranger's face
It soothes me to know
That what I say matters
Just for a moment
And when that moment passes
I will still be searching
For the right words.

9

I have never been called a warrior
Does this mean I am not strong?
Perhaps words are like lipstick for the soul
And 'Warrior' is not my shade
But I wear it anyway.

10

I once knew a girl who had all the answers
Sometimes I still see her
But now, she is silent
Like a bon fire that is done burning
Years ago, I set out to look for her
But the world tells me she never existed
Maybe it's true
There's no proof
Nothing but my memories
And even they lie
Like ashes at the foot of a fire
Cold and white and fine as when I say I'm okay
The wind steals them
An invisible menace
Like the girl who haunts my heart.

11

Simply said
Your words
Run deep
These cuts
They weep
Long nights
We fight
To be
Seen twice
In black
Then white
Our lips
Sewn shut
We sleep
Wake up
To see
The ghosts
Are gone
But we
Are haunted.

12

Every day, the ocean steals a grain of sand from the beach
Or maybe she surrenders them willingly
Like souvenirs to a weary traveler
We're all beaches, I think
Giving pieces of ourselves away
Never knowing where they end up
While life comes and goes around us
Gently pulling us back
To the place where we belong.

Love's not blind
It's the chances taken in a fit of over-confidence
The warmth wished for in the dark
Slow sips by the low light of every bright idea we never had
the courage to chase
Songs that never sounded so good
Or made so much sense
Words we never had the strength to say
Can suddenly move mountains
After midnight, nothing matters
And everything breaks
Stumbling into bed, we fall
Knowing that dreams will catch us
Love's not blind
It's drunk
Blushing, crying, screaming
Our laughter is a lie
The pain lives on
To drown another day.

Nothing to say
But still, you talk
And talk
I pray for silence
You reach for the bottle, freeing the genie
My wish, granted
Just a little more, you say
But more is never enough
Wings clipped, the caged songbird sings
And reminisces
About blue skies and open spaces
Now she's a prisoner
To red walls and oak barrels
Each mellow note carrying her far away
Up to the heavens
To be free
Forever.

White,
> the colour of her dress on the happiest day of her life

Cream,
> the colour of the sheets where two become one

Champagne,
> the colour of the complimentary bubbly

Yellow,
> the colour of the soup sprayed across the walls

Amber,
> the colour of his justification

Cherry,
> the colour of her blood as she picks up the pieces

Crimson,
> the colour of his latest apology

Shiraz,
> the colour of her only solace

Orchid,
> the colour of her wrist beneath her sleeve

Moss,

      the colour of his eyes up close

Forest,

      the colour of the carpet at the first motel she finds

Slate,

      the colour of the room when he calls her home

Silver,

      the colour of the handcuffs behind his back

Black,

      the colour of her mother's dress on the saddest day

      of her life.

So much darkness left to cover
And you're not here to walk me through it
The end of the road for you was just the beginning
Of the longest journey of my life
Even in death
I guess there's something to look forward to
And that's seeing you again
I won't ask you to wait; that seems unfair
There's a lot of darkness to cover in the cosmos
Where the strands of stardust that once made you whole
Have unraveled
And so have I
So will I.

If you must love me
If you feel you have no other choice but to be the bearer of
my broken pieces
Promise me you will never name a star in my honour
Love doesn't speak the language of the galaxy
Leave the flowers in the field untouched
To grow and flourish as they may
If you feel my name is worthy of a sacrifice
Let it be a slice of time on your life's clock
Or the bite of pie you swore you didn't want
So I can let its sweetness linger
And feed it back to you with the lights off
Please don't tell me I'm the one
Unless you're prepared to love the million versions of me that
came before
And the millions that are yet to come
This is my promise to you, if there was ever one
worth making
I will never ask more than I'm willing to give
And I will leave every star unnamed
So that our love will truly be
Universal.

Lately you've been
Under my skin
The way I was once
              under

                      yours
Limbs tightly hinged
A prisoner by necessity
Is there any part of me
              that looks

                      like you?
If not the crowbar under the sofa
Or the shoes in the cab, blissfully forgotten
Then maybe
              we are both

                      broken
We are not the same woman
But our eyes and our hair match
I'm afraid to ask
              what else

                      we share.
*

I didn't throw salt over my shoulder tonight
Dinner for two waits on the stove
There may
              never be

                      a third
But at least the floor is clean
Maybe I should try it

Throw some salt
        For luck
                Or just because
It beats painting camels on the wall
One hump or two? You never told me
And now I wonder
        Why a camel
                In the kitchen?
*

It comes back to the lemon tree
It's all in my head, they say, and they're right
I live here
        with you
                and without
We're both wearing denim overalls
And your magazines are still missing
But at least
        they
                are together.

I have OCD
But sometimes, it owns me
I count things that don't require counting
I put off writing because I'm afraid of the mistakes I haven't
yet made
I wonder why no one has called
But sit in silence for hours
And cry
A simple oversight can render me immobile
I've seen more of the ceiling than my family
They don't understand
And neither do I
Some things in life are too strange for words
So I stick to numbers instead
Like three, five, and ten, if I'm feeling patient
But never four or six, unless they're together
Don't ask me to come and clean your house
That's not what the 'c' stands for
It means that the counterclockwise motion of the dish
sponge
Feels like a burden and an obligation
As satisfying as a drug, but harder to quit
My hands shake if I try
Like I'm in withdrawal from myself
Addicts of the irrational are we
The ones with the bloody hands and the bulletproof rituals
Proof that even control can be chaos.

22

I stopped counting
Nothing adds up
This veil of sadness
Feels more like a bag over my head
Muffled screams in a plastic void
Just breathe, they say
It's only life
There's always tomorrow
A different day
A new number
But I'm still one person
And I am
Shattered beyond repair.

Each morning, I am unceremoniously reborn
Lured into the light by the clock's fingerless hands
It is rarely a gentle transition
Nonetheless, I rise
All is quiet, as it should be
And there's no one to tell me
That I need to speak up
I'm already up, and that's enough
It seems discourteous to worry at such a juvenile hour
So instead, I wonder
And I write
Do certain words ever wish they were other words?
Do they look at their neighbour and covet their simplicity or
grandiloquence?
Or do they just accept their place on the page?
They must know they were created for a reason
Be words, I tell myself
But I think
I already am.

Please check on me. I don't want to be a burden.
So much advice I don't need, like plastic in the ocean.
Your words in rings around my neck.
Can't you see I'm dying yet?

It starts with friction
For you, I burn
Like a smile in the dark
You feast on my warmth
Our bodies so close
That your breath makes me shudder
To you, I am just a match
A blazing beacon of hope
To light the road ahead
From my primordial crown
To my wooden stem
I give you everything I have
For the chance to be carried
Into the night.

I used to think I could do anything
Now everything feels like a chore
And I'm sinking
The ocean and the sky
Are both blue and endless
But one is wide and free
And the other is cold and dark
They meet each other in the middle
Without ever touching
Dry land tucked between their mysteries
I'm not sure if there's a point to this
The analogy or the writing
But the words come like rain
Falling where they please
Making a home wherever they land
Or if not
They find their way
I can only hope that one day, I will join them
Be one with whatever shade of blue
I drift towards
I like that word: drifting
Momentum without urgency
Direction without purpose
What a privilege it is to be carried
By a force greater than ourselves
The leaves are changing
And I bet they aren't afraid
Falling together

Taking up space with their colours
Layers upon layers of life
Peacefully embracing the passage of time
A gift to the eye
An ode to infinity.

Jessica Ingold is the author of three books for young adult readers as well as countless blogs and newspaper articles. With over ten years of experience in writing and self-publishing, her goal is to craft stories that resonate with book enthusiasts of all ages. *Quiet* is her first book of poetry.

Twitter.com/JessieIngold
Facebook.com/jessingoldbooks
Lulu.com/spotlight/jessicaingold